Anonymous

Leith Hill and Wotton House

Anonymous

Leith Hill and Wotton House

ISBN/EAN: 9783337890896

Printed in Europe, USA, Canada, Australia, Japan

Cover: Foto ©Andreas Hilbeck / pixelio.de

More available books at **www.hansebooks.com**

LEITH HILL

AND

WOTTON HOUSE.

Leith Hill and Wotton.

We are requested by Mr. Evelyn to make it known that Leith Hill Tower will be open to the public on every Saturday during the present year from May 7th to September 24th (both inclusive) between the hours of 2 p.m. and 6 30 p.m.

In the beginning of the year Mr. Evelyn notified his intention that the House and Grounds at Wotton should be opened on the same days. Owing to some repairs not yet completed, this cannot take place till the end of May; after which date, on every Saturday from June 4th till September 24th, (both inclusive,) Visitors will be admitted to see the House and Grounds from 10 30 a.m. till 6 p.m., except from 1 p.m till 2 p.m.

Any Person wishing to see the House and Grounds should apply to us for an order at least one day previously; no party should consist of more than 5 persons; carriages may drive as far as the Gate-house. On calling at the House Visitors are requested to enter their Names in a Visitors' Book.

The present House and Grounds retain the general character they bore in John Evelyn's time. Parts of the old building still remain and the present proprietor is naturally desirous of meeting the wishes of those who feel an interest in seeing the place where the author of "Sylva & Terra" was born and where he died. In the Library may be noticed Portraits of John Evelyn, by Nanteuil, Walker, and Kneller, a Bible annotated by him, King Charles I's Prayerbook, Sketches of Wotton drawn by John Evelyn, &c., &c.

In the Picture Gallery will be exhibited Pictures once belonging to John Evelyn's Collection.

The Monumental Chancel in Wotton Church will be open on every Sunday, from May till September (inclusive): the chief objects of general interest there are the Tombs of John Evelyn and his Wife.

HART, HART & MARTEN.

As Leith Hill Tower and Wotton House are objects of interest in the neighbourhood of Dorking, the following brief notice of these two spots may be interesting to such persons as may visit the neighbourhood.

LEITH HILL TOWER, & c.

The summit of Leith Hill, nearly a thousand feet high, the most elevated spot in the south east of England, is situated five miles from Dorking, and is crowned by a Prospect Tower, commanding an extensive view over portions of Surrey, Sussex, Hants, Berks, Oxford, Buckingham, Hertford, Middlesex, Essex, Kent, and, by the aid of a glass, Wiltshire. On a clear day the heights of Highgate and the roofs of the Crystal Palace at Sydenham may be seen. The View from Leith Hill was admired by the Author of the Sylva, and is thought by many to surpass that from the Apennines over Valdamo, or that from Tivoli over the Campagna.

The Tower was completed in 1766, by Richard Hull, Esq., of Leith Hill Place, on a part of the waste

4

ground of Wotton Manor, granted to him by Sir John
Evelyn, Bart., on certain conditions. It bears on the
West side the following inscription.

Ut teram undique beatam
Videas viator
Hæc turris de longe spectabilis
Sumptibus Richardi Hull
Ex agro Leith Hill Place, Arm.
Exstructa fuit
Oblectamento non sui solum
Sed vicinorum
Et omnium.

"That, you, traveller, may see the Country happy on
every side, this tower visible from afar was built at the
expense of Richard Hull, Esq., of Leith Hill Place, in
the reign of George III. A.D., 1766, as a source of de-
'light, not only to himself but to his neighbours and
everybody."

Mr. Hull, was by his own direction buried under
the Tower: and within the building on the East wall
was 🌸 a Tablet of Portland stone thus inscribed,

"Underneath this floor lieth the body of
RICHARD HULL, ESQ.,
a native of Bristol,
who departed this life, January 18th, 1772,
in the 83rd year of his age."

For many years after the building of the Tower it was
open to the public in accordance with the intention of
Mr. Hull: the privilege however was thought to be
abused, and it was said that the Tower had become a
harbour for vagrants and smugglers. So about the year
1800, a subscription having been raised among the
neighbouring gentry, the entrance door was built up ˄
and the whole interior of the Tower filled with stone
and cement: and it was found in this state when, a few
years ago, the Tower and the land adjoining were
purchased by ˄the present lord of the Manor. So solid
was the Cement that it was found impossible to re-open
the old entrance and interior staircase: therefore a
staircase-tower was built by the side of the old tower,
in order to make the building available for its original
purpose,

WOTTON HOUSE, &c.

Wotton House is an irregular and heterogeneous mass
of buildings and outhouses chiefly interesting as having
been the birth place of John Evelyn the celebrated
author of the Sylva, who was here born October 31,
1620, and whose tomb is to be seen in Wotton Church.

In the new Library built in 1864, after the design
of H. Woodyer, Esq., on the site of the West wing

(destroyed by fire about 1800) may be seen various family and local relics and among these the three extant portraits of John Evelyn. As however the objects of interest are labelled there is no need of describing them here.

THE PICTURE GALLERY.

In the new Picture Gallery are placed the most interesting of the Pictures that yet remain of John Evelyn's collection.

THE DRAWING ROOM.

The Drawing Room was built by Sir Frederick Evelyn Bart., after the fire which consumed the West wing of the House. Several of the pictures now in the Drawing Room are family portraits of no general interest.

On the West wall the large portrait is that of Prince George of Denmark husband of Queen Anne. On the right is that of Sarah the famous duchess of Marlborough.

On the South wall are various family portraits. The centre portrait West of the fire place is of a gentleman Age 57. A. D. 1596.

On the East wall of the Drawing Room is a large portrait (by Sir Martin Shee) of John Evelyn, Esq., of Wotton who succeeded to the Wotton Estate in 1814, bequeathed to him by Lady Evelyn widow of Sir Frederick Evelyn Bart. On the right of this portrait is that of Mrs. Godolphin her left hand resting on a slab supporting an urn. Mrs. Godolphin is often affectionately mentioned by John Evelyn in the Diary and elsewhere. Her life from a M S written by John Evelyn has been edited by the present Bishop of Winchester (Wilberforce) In the Library may be noticed a bible annotated by John Evelyn to be given " after my decease to Mary Blagge since the wife of Sidney Godolphin, Esq., if she survive me ". On the left of the portrait by Sir Martin Shee is that of Lady Godolphin and her son.

In the Drawing-room ~~Room~~ (East side) under a picture of a serpent, butterfly, &c. is a view of Ballinacourty county Tipperary Ireland (1831.) the seat of James Hewitt Massy Dawson, Esq., and now (1870.) of his son George Massy Dawson, Esq.; in the ~~Room~~' (West side) is a Picture of a Stray Sheep on a common by Redgrave; R.A. the scene is taken from Abinger Common near Wotton,

THE DINING ROOM.

The Dining-room is old and with the Entrance-hall was probably altered in 1646. Next to the entrance door from the Drawing Room is a portrait of Sir Frederick

Evelyn, on a grey horse. The horses and dogs in this room belonged to Sir Frederick Evelyn, and are drawn by Gilpin. Among them is a picture of Sir Frederick's favorite horse Ploughboy (a grey horse with a groom.)

The other Pictures in this room are from John Evelyn's collection. Among them are several by Hemskirk.

Behind the Colonnade is a semicircle of Portraits— Archbishop Tillotson, Lady Godolphin, the Earl of Godolphin, &c. Opposite to Tillotson and next to the garden door is a portrait of John Evelyn's son John, holding a book in his hand.

THE GARDEN, &c.

The Garden and garden front of the house are much the same as in the time of Evelyn, as will be seen on comparison with John Evelyn's own drawings in the library.

The Mount cut into terraces, the Temple or "grotto" with its portico, the fountain, &c. are mentioned in the Diary. Below what is now the Swimming-bath, and on the right side of the stream is the spot where John Evelyn built "a study" in his youthful days.

The Estate of Wotton continued in the hands of John Evelyn's direct descendants till the year 1812, when Sir Frederick Evelyn dying without issue bequeathed the estate to his widow and she dying in 1814 returned the estate to the family by bequeathing it to John Evelyn, Esq., (whose portrait by Sir Martin Shee, is in the drawing room) descended from George Evelyn of Wotton (the first purchaser of the Estate) through Sir John Evelyn Knight of Godstone, the former being the grandfather, the latter the kinsman and friend of the author of " Sylva ".

www.ingramcontent.com/pod-product-compliance
Lightning Source LLC
Chambersburg PA
CBHW021611270326
41931CB00009B/1436